THE 13 AMENDMENTS OF THE US CONSTITUTION

Government Books 7th Grade Children's Government Books

An addition or change to the United States Constitution is known as an amendment. The Bill of Rights consists of the first ten amendments to the Constitution. Read further to learn about how an amendment becomes part of the Constitution and also about the 13 Amendments of the US Constitution.

How are Amendments to the Constitution Made?

The process to make an amendment to the Constitution consists of two steps:

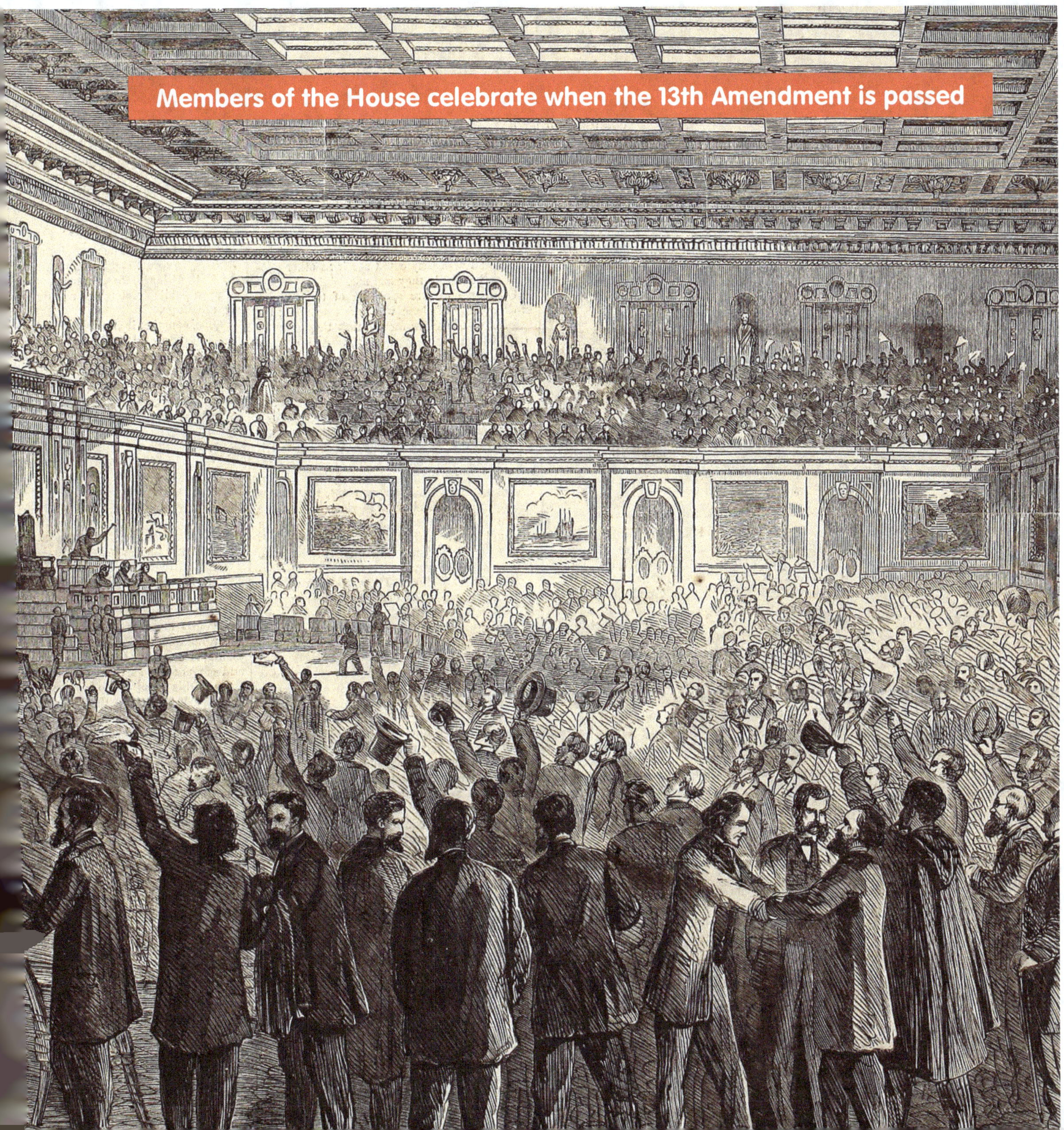
Members of the House celebrate when the 13th Amendment is passed

The United States Capitol

Step 1: Proposal – An amendment will be proposed either by a national convention consisting of two-thirds of the states, or a two-thirds vote by Congress, which includes the Senate and the House of Representatives. Currently, all of the amendments have been proposed by Congress.

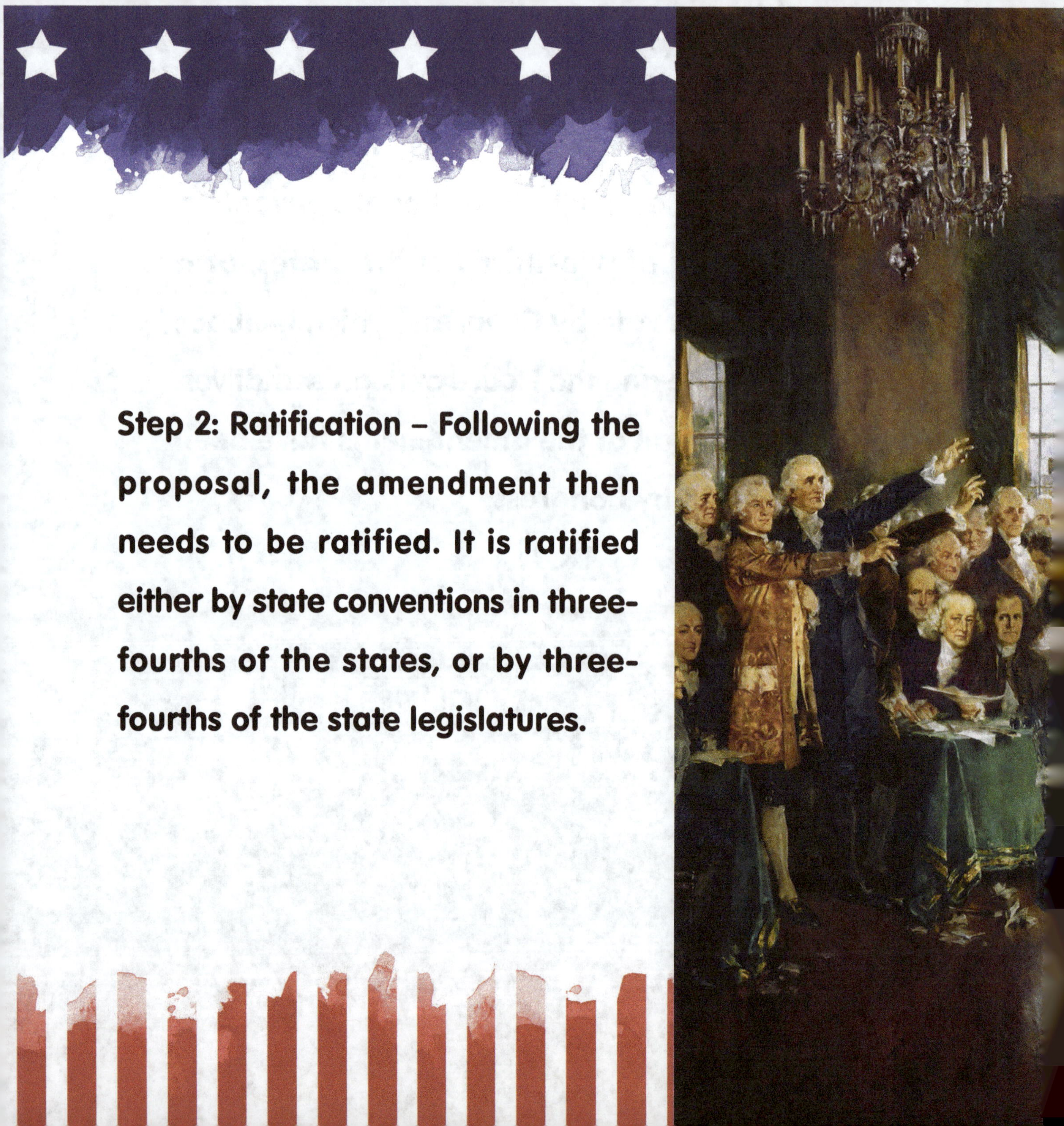

Step 2: Ratification – Following the proposal, the amendment then needs to be ratified. It is ratified either by state conventions in three-fourths of the states, or by three-fourths of the state legislatures.

Signing of the Constitution

The Bill of Rights

Amendment I
Congress shall make no law respecting an establishment of religion, or prohibiting the free exercise thereof; or abridging the freedom of speech, or of the press; or the right of the people peaceably to assemble, and to petition the Government for a redress of grievances.

Amendment II
A well regulated Militia, being necessary to the security of a free State, the right of the people to keep and bear Arms, shall not be infringed.

Amendment III
No Soldier shall, in time of peace be quartered in any house, without the consent of the Owner, nor in time of war, but in a manner to be prescribed by law.

Amendment IV
The right of the people to be secure in their persons, houses, papers, and effects, against unreasonable searches and seizures, shall not be violated, and no Warrants shall issue, but upon probable cause, supported by Oath or affirmation, and particularly describing the place to be searched, and the persons or things to be seized.

Amendment V
No person shall be held to answer for a capital, or otherwise infamous crime, unless on a presentment or indictment of a Grand Jury, except in cases arising in the land or naval forces, or in the Militia, when in actual service in time of War or public danger; nor shall any person be subject for the same offence to be twice put in jeopardy of life or limb; nor shall be compelled in any criminal case to be a witness against himself, nor be deprived of life, liberty, or property, without due process of law; nor shall private property be taken for public use, without just compensation.

Amendment VI
In all criminal prosecutions, the accused shall enjoy the right to a speedy and public trial, by an impartial jury of the State and district wherein the crime shall have been committed, which district shall have been previously ascertained by law, and to be informed of the nature and cause of the accusation; to be confronted with the witnesses against him; to have compulsory process for obtaining witnesses in his favor, and to have the Assistance of Counsel for his defence.

Amendment VII
In Suits at common law, where the value in controversy shall exceed twenty dollars, the right of trial by jury shall be preserved, and no fact tried by a jury, shall be otherwise re-examined in any Court of the United States, than according to the rules of the common law.

Amendment VIII
Excessive bail shall not be required, nor excessive fines imposed, nor cruel and unusual punishments inflicted.

Amendment IX
The enumeration in the Constitution, of certain rights, shall not be construed to deny or disparage others retained by the people.

Amendment X
The powers not delegated to the United States by the Constitution, nor prohibited by it to the States, are reserved to the States respectively, or to the people.

JUDICIAL CONFERENCE OF THE UNITED STATES
COMMITTEE ON THE BICENTENNIAL OF THE CONSTITUTION

Damon J. Keith
Chairman

Dec. 15, 1791 - Dec. 15, 1991

Bill of Rights Plaque

THE BILL OF RIGHTS

The first 10 Amendments to the Constitution of the United States are known as the Bill of Rights. The theory behind this was to ensure citizens of America certain rights and freedom. It limited the power of government in what they could do and what they could control.

Freedoms included the freedom of speech, religion, assembly, the right to bear arms, the right to a speedy trial, unreasonable search and seizure of your private home, and several others.

Freedom of Speech

We the Peop[le]

insure domestic Tranquility
and our Posterity, do ordain

Article

Section 1. All legislative Powers herein granted

Many state delegates were not amicable to signing the Constitution without the inclusion of the Bill of Rights. This would become a major issue with some states in ratifying the Constitution.

Because of this, James Madison proceeded to write 12 amendments and in 1789, he presented them in front of the First Congress. Ten of the 12 amendments passed on December 15, 1791, and made a part of our Constitution. These would later be referred to as the Bill of Rights.

James Madison

Bill of Rights Memorial

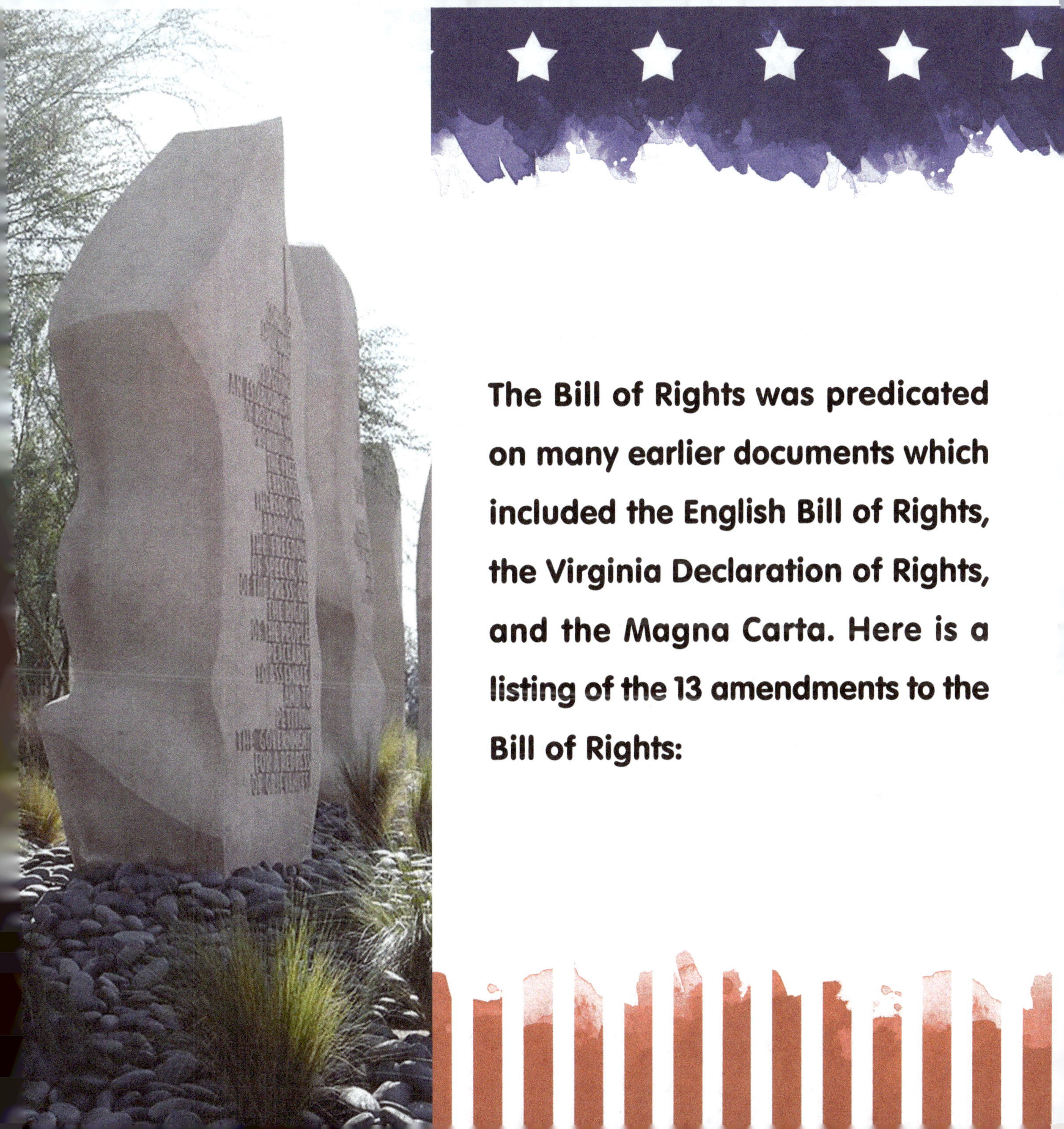

The Bill of Rights was predicated on many earlier documents which included the English Bill of Rights, the Virginia Declaration of Rights, and the Magna Carta. Here is a listing of the 13 amendments to the Bill of Rights:

The First Amendment states that Congress shall not make any law that prevents the establishment of a religion or prohibit its freedom. It also protects freedom of assembly, freedom of speech, freedom of the press, and the right to petition the Government for a redress of complaints.

First Amendment Inscription
CONGRESS SHALL MAKE NO LAW respecting
an establishment of religion, or prohibiting the free
exercise thereof; or abridging the freedom of speech,
or of the press; or the right of the people peaceably
to assemble, and to petition the Government for a
redress of grievances.
THE FIRST AMENDMENT
TO THE U.S. CONSTITUTION
15 December 1791

GRIP ZONE
MADE PROUDLY
ALIEN GEAR

The Second Amendment protects our rights as a citizen to bear arms. This amendment has become very controversial recently. Some people would like additional laws preventing citizens from owning guns. They believe this might help stop shootings as well as preventing criminals and mentally ill people from obtaining guns. Others want to retain this right and make sure that it is not limited. They believe that possessing guns provides them with protection from criminals as well as a rise of a tyrannical government.

Although this amendment allows people ownership of guns, it does not, however, prevent regulation by the government. Gun laws are created to keep criminals and mentally ill people from obtaining guns. Also, they assist in keeping track of guns and note what kinds of guns citizens are permitted to own.

We the People
of the United States
Article 1

Nuclear Bomb Explosion

Some weapons, such as a nuclear bomb, should not be owned by the public. The difficulty is trying to find out where to draw the line. Currently, this creates much debate in American politics.

The Third Amendment stops the government from putting troops in private homes. As you first read this amendment, you probably wonder why our Founding Fathers decided on adding it. It was actually a major problem during the Revolutionary War. The British had passed laws known as the Quartering Acts which allowed their soldiers to be able to take the homes of American colonists.

Quartering Acts

Federal Government Building of the United States

The Third Amendment has not come into play much in our modern times. On occasion, there have been some wars occurring on American soil where the government provides for housing for our soldiers. It has been used to provide for a citizen's privacy rights by indicating that the government does not have the right to enter private property without the owner's consent.

The Fourth Amendment stops the government from being able to unreasonably search and seize property of a United States Citizens. It requires a warrant be issued by a judge and that there is probable cause for the warrant.

Revolutionary War

This amendment was a result of action of the British tax collectors prior to the Revolutionary War. They used general warrants for entering and searching any house that they wanted to without the need of any evidence of criminal activity. The Founding Fathers sought protection for citizens from this type of privacy invasion by the government.

The Fifth Amendment is most known for people quoting it as "I'll take the Fifth". This provides a citizen with the right to decide whether or not they want to testify in a court of law if they believe that their testimony might implicate themselves. This amendment also protects citizens from being subject to prosecution and punishment of a crime with no due process.

Courtroom

The amendment also states that a person cannot be tried more than once for the same crime. It also establishes power of eminent domain, meaning that private property can't be seized for public use with compensation that is just. Originally applying to only federal court cases, it now applies to state courts through the Fourteenth Amendment.

The Sixth Amendment provides guarantee of a speedy trial including a jury of your peers. It also states that the accused have to be apprised of the crime for which they are being charged and that they have the right of confronting the witnesses brought forth by the government. In addition, it provides an accused person the right to demand testimony by witnesses, as well as to having legal representation, meaning that government has to provide counsel.

Jury

The Seventh Amendment states that all civil cases shall be tried by a jury. The Founding Fathers wanted to ensure that government would not omit trial by jury as they had concerns that if cases were decided only by the judge, he might side with government, which would provide government with too much control. This occurred to colonists when judges, appointed by a king, would side with the king every time. They believe that a jury of local citizens would more likely provide a fair trial.

The Eighth Amendment protects against excessive fines, excessive bail, and cruel and unusual punishment.

Supreme Court

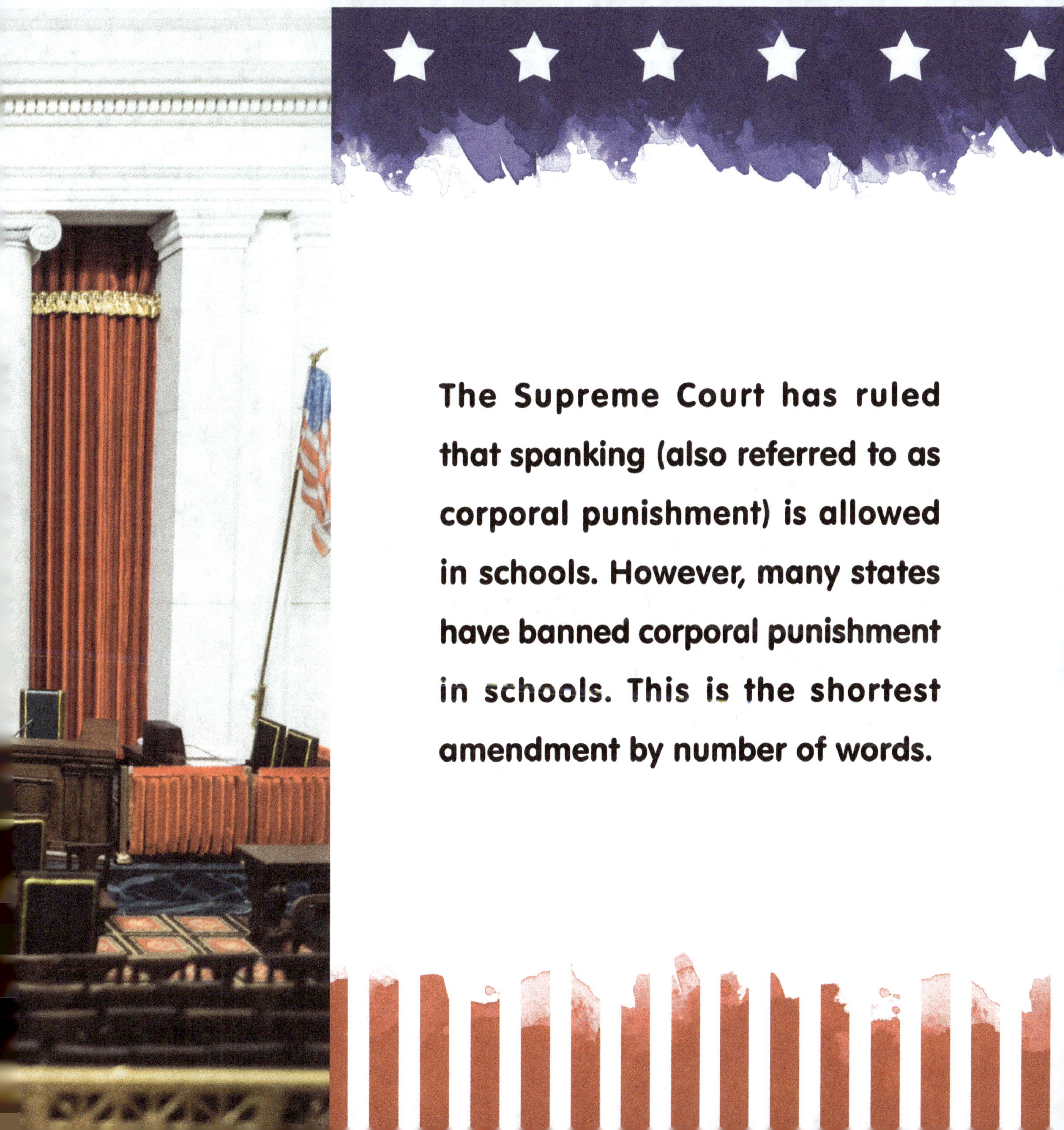

The Supreme Court has ruled that spanking (also referred to as corporal punishment) is allowed in schools. However, many states have banned corporal punishment in schools. This is the shortest amendment by number of words.

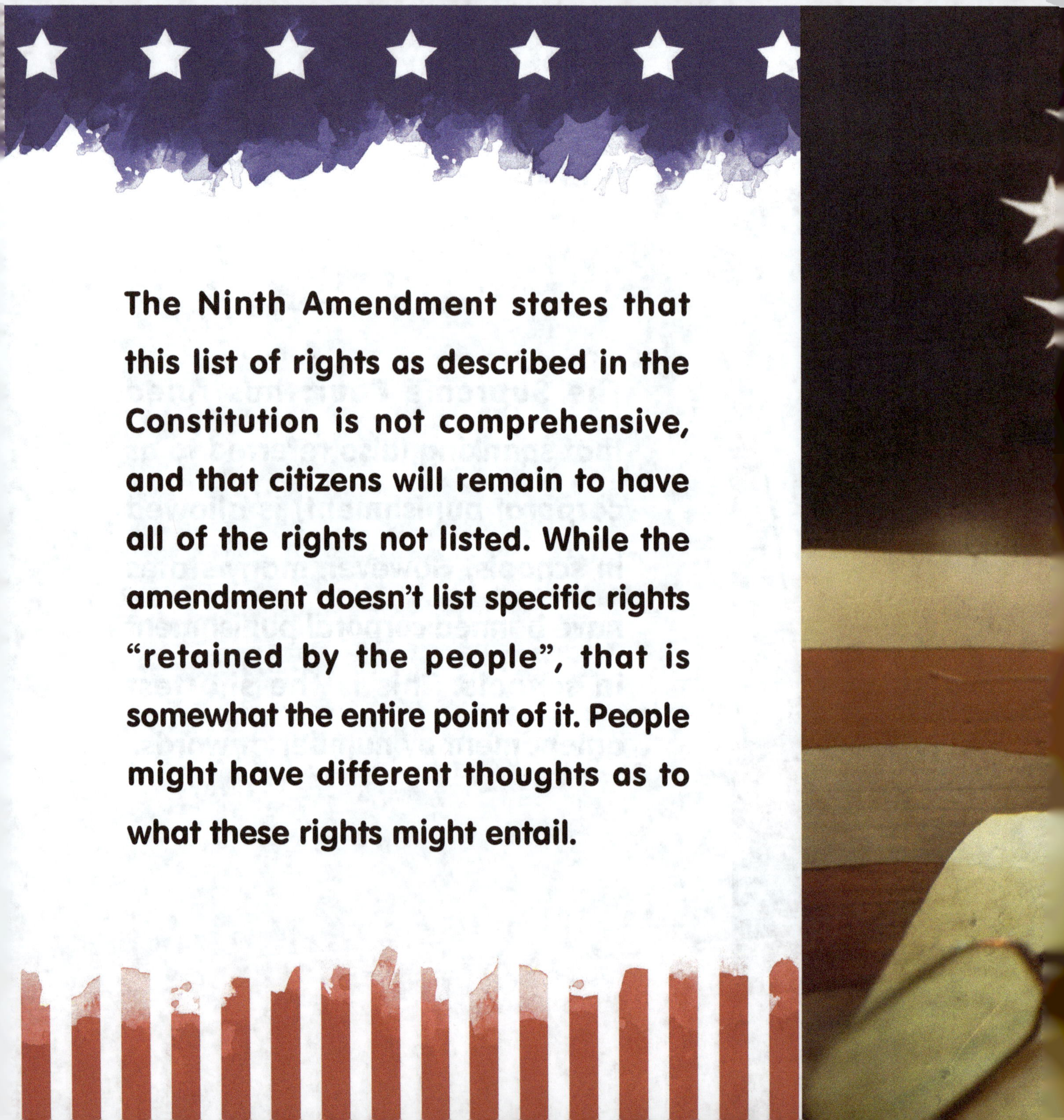

The Ninth Amendment states that this list of rights as described in the Constitution is not comprehensive, and that citizens will remain to have all of the rights not listed. While the amendment doesn't list specific rights "retained by the people", that is somewhat the entire point of it. People might have different thoughts as to what these rights might entail.

We the People
insure domestic Tranquility provide for the common defence,
and our Posterity, do ordain and establish this Constitution
Article 1
of the U

United States Capitol

The Tenth Amendment provides all of the powers not given specifically to the government in the Constitution, either to the people or to the states. The US was created as a group of states with one federal government. The federal government has powers provided to it under the Constitution, while state governments have the remaining power, along with the citizens. This amendment was added to make sure the powers held by the federal government continue to be limited. The writers of this amendment wanted it to be understood that the federal government's power stems from the states and the people.

The Eleventh Amendment, ratified on February 7, 1795, set the limits on when it's possible to sue a state. Particularly, giving immunity to states from citizens out-of-state, as well as foreigners not residing within that particular state's border.

SUPREME COURT
SUPREME COURT OF FLORIDA
Supreme Court

A suit can always be brought against a state's subdivisions, including municipalities, cities and counties. A state is permitted to agree to a lawsuit against it in a federal court. Congress can remove the state's immunity from a suit in federal court, if its intention to remove the immunity is "unmistakably clear".

The Twelfth Amendment, ratified on June 15, 1804, revised procedures for the presidential elections. This amendment introduced the Electoral College system, still in force today. It was originally intended to be an emergency fix during the 1804 elections following the previous two elections, 1796 and 1800, that were horribly wrong.

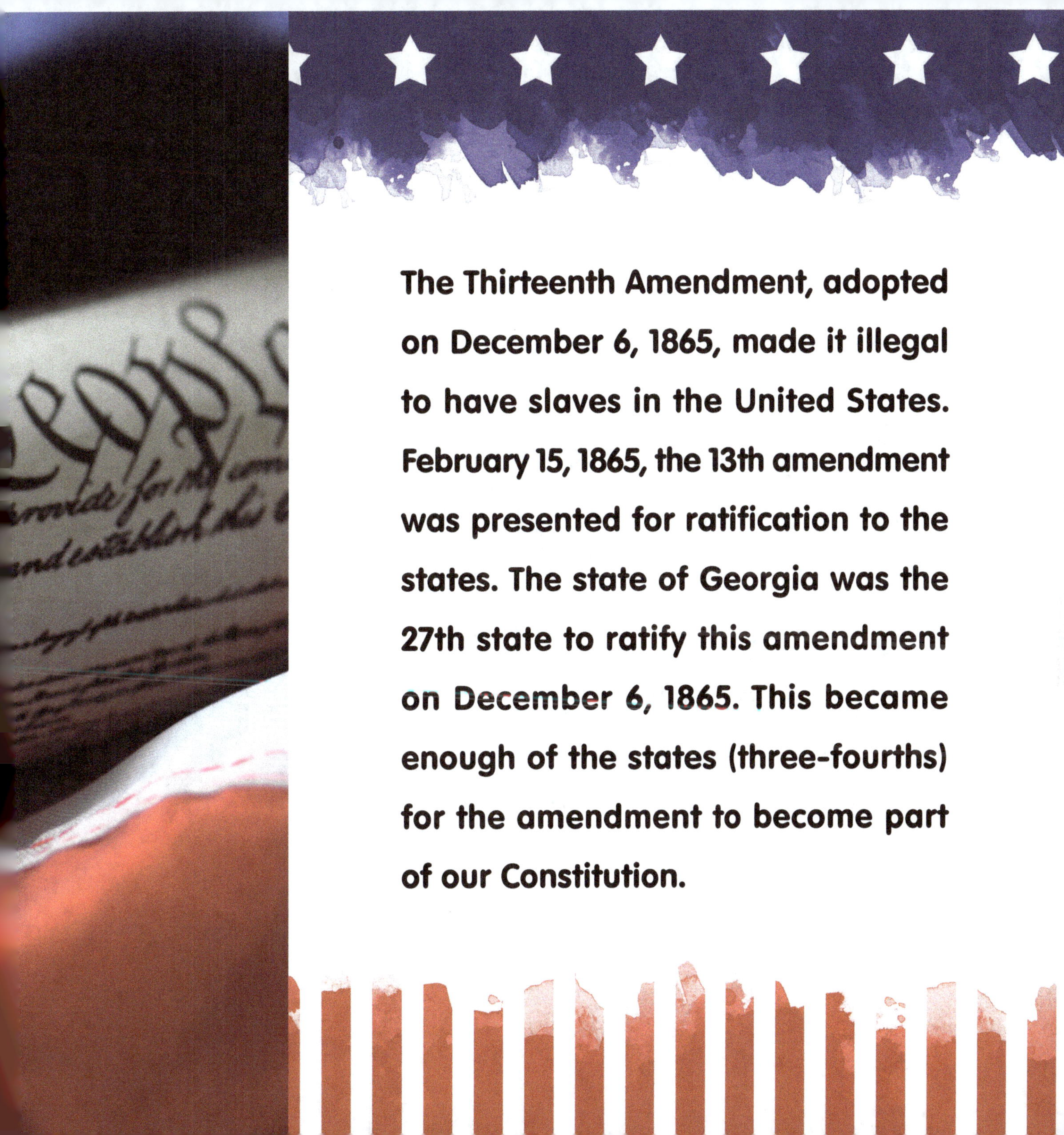

The Thirteenth Amendment, adopted on December 6, 1865, made it illegal to have slaves in the United States. February 15, 1865, the 13th amendment was presented for ratification to the states. The state of Georgia was the 27th state to ratify this amendment on December 6, 1865. This became enough of the states (three-fourths) for the amendment to become part of our Constitution.

There are currently 27 amendments to the Constitution with the last one being ratified in 1992. To learn more about the Bill of Rights, the Constitution, and its amendments, you can go to your local library, research the internet, and ask questions of your teachers, family and friends.

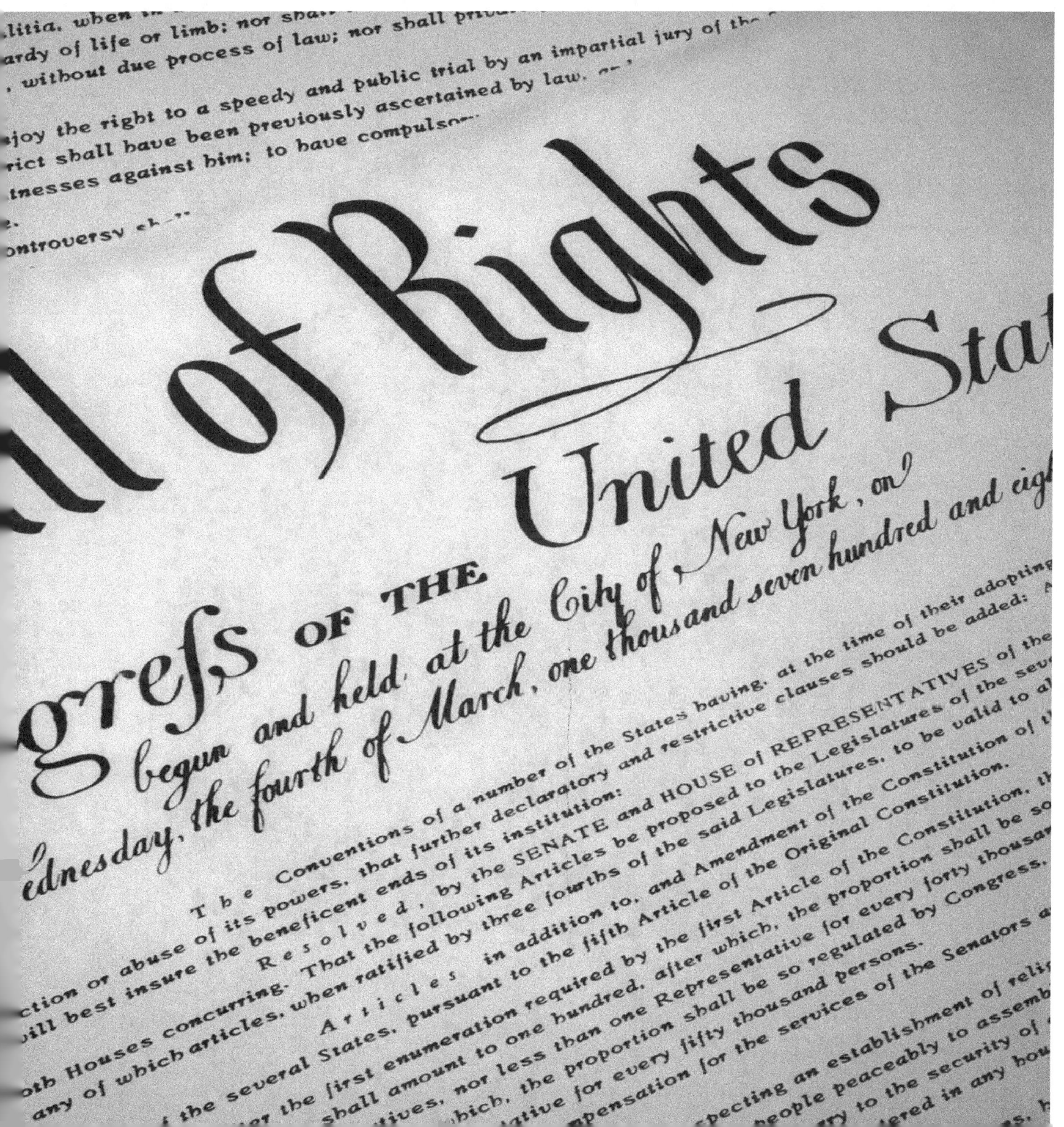

ilitia, when in ... nor shal...
ardy of life or limb; nor shall priv...
, without due process of law; nor shall ...
joy the right to a speedy and public trial by an impartial jury of the
rict shall have been previously ascertained by law, and
tnesses against him; to have compulso...
e.
ontroversy sh...

ll of Rights
gress OF THE United Stat
begun and held at the City of New York, on
ednesday, the fourth of March, one thousand seven hundred and eig

The Conventions of a number of the States having, at the time of their adopting
ction or abuse of its powers, that further declaratory and restrictive clauses should be added: A
ill best insure the beneficent ends of its institution:
Resolved, by the SENATE and HOUSE of REPRESENTATIVES of the
oth Houses concurring. That the following Articles be proposed to the Legislatures of the sev
any of which articles, when ratified by three fourths of the said Legislatures, to be valid to al
Articles in addition to, and Amendment of the Constitution of t
the several States, pursuant to the fifth Article of the Original Constitution.
er the first enumeration required by the first Article of the Constitution, th
shall amount to one hundred, after which, the proportion shall be so
tives, nor less than one Representative for every forty thousan
hich, the proportion shall be so regulated by Congress,
tative for every fifty thousand persons.
pensation for the services of the Senators a
specting an establishment of reli
people peaceably to assemb
ry to the security of
tered in any hou

Visit
BABY PROFESSOR
EDUCATION KIDS
www.BabyProfessorBooks.com
to download Free Baby Professor eBooks
and view our catalog of new and exciting
Children's Books